FOOTBALL SUPERSTARS

SALAH
RULES

Hi, pleased to meet you.

We hope you enjoy our book about Mo Salah!

I'm **VARbot** with all the facts and stats!

SIMON

DAN

WELBECK

VAR

THIS IS A WELBECK CHILDREN'S BOOK
Published in 2021 by Welbeck Children's Books Limited
An imprint of the Welbeck Publishing Group
20 Mortimer Street, London W1T 3JW
Text © 2021 Simon Mugford
Design & Illustration © 2021 Dan Green
ISBN: 978-1-78312-564-7

Writer: Simon Mugford
Designer and Illustrator: Dan Green
Design manager: Sam James
Executive editor: Suhel Ahmed
Production: Freencky Portas

A catalogue record for this book is available from the British Library.

Printed in the UK
2 4 6 8 10 9 7 5 3

Statistics and records correct as of November 2020

FOOTBALL SUPERSTARS

SALAH

RULES

SIMON MUGFORD   DAN GREEN

CONTENTS

SALAH! SALAH!

Mohamed Salah is one of the best footballers in the world. The **Egyptian superstar** with a huge smile has won the **CHAMPIONS LEAGUE** and **PREMIER LEAGUE** with **Liverpool** and is an idol for millions of fans in **Africa** and across the world.

THIS BOOK IS ALL ABOUT HIM!

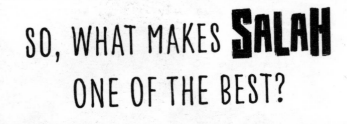

SO, WHAT MAKES **SALAH** ONE OF THE BEST?

Speed
Super-quick, with incredible bursts of acceleration.

Dribbling
Brilliant at getting past defenders with the ball at his feet.

Finishing
Cool in front of goal. When he shoots he's almost always on target.

First touch
Salah's first touch of the ball is world class.

GOALS!
Best of all, **SALAH** scores goals – **LOTS** and **LOTS** of them!

SALAH IN NUMBERS

So, **how good** is **Mo Salah?**

Let's look at some **numbers:**

1 ...PREMIER LEAGUE win

1 ...CHAMPIONS LEAGUE win

2 ...PREMIER LEAGUE Golden Boots

1 ...Players' Player of the Year Award

1

. . . Premier League Player of the Season Award

Over

100 GOALS

for **Liverpool**

Estimated

£100

MILLION transfer value

Over **40 MILLION**

followers on Instagram.

MO SALAH I.D.

NAME:
Mohamed Salah Hamed Mahrous Ghaly

NICKNAME:
The Pharaoh, The Egyptian King

DATE OF BIRTH:
15 June 1992

PLACE OF BIRTH: *Nagrig, Egypt*

HEIGHT: *1.75 m*

POSITION: *Forward/Right winger*

CLUBS: *El Mokawloon, Basel, Chelsea, Fiorentina (on loan), Roma, Liverpool*

NATIONAL TEAM: *Egypt*

LEFT OR RIGHT-FOOTED: *Left*

CHAPTER 2

VILLAGE LIFE

Mohamed Salah was born in **1992** in a small farming village in **Egypt** called **Nagrig.**

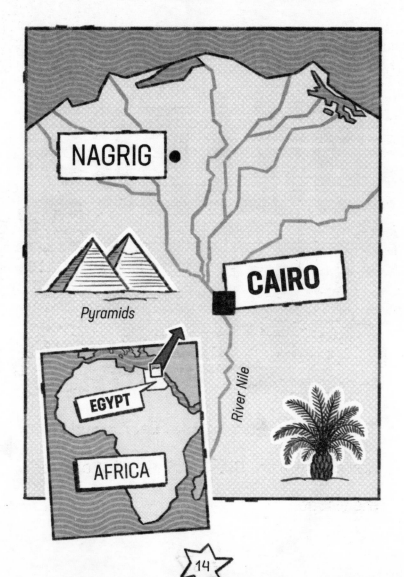

NAGRIG

CAIRO

Pyramids

EGYPT

AFRICA

River Nile

The people of **Nagrig** are **VERY** proud of Salah. There are **pictures of him** all over the village.

Mohamed lived in **Nagrig** with his mum and dad, and his younger brother, **Nasr.**

There was one thing that **Mo** and **Nasr** loved more than anything else . . .

PLAYING FOOTBALL!

There was one **dry, dusty football pitch** in the centre of Nagrig. Mo and Nasr spent **ALL** of their spare time playing football with the other boys in the village.

When Salah had the ball, nobody could catch him - not even the **big boys!**

When Mo was **12,** his dad took him for a **trial** with **Ittihad Basyoun,** a football club about **half an hour's** drive from Nagrig.

Mo was very **nervous,** but once he got the ball - **BOOM** - he was off! Nobody could stop him!

YOUR SON IS **FANTASTIC.**

Young Mo would watch **Champions League** matches with his friends in a café in Nagrig. He dreamed of being a **superstar player** like . . .

Zinedine Zidane - *French midfield maestro*

Ronaldo - *Brazilian super striker*

Mo has always had a **big smile** and a big heart. As a boy he would feed the **stray dogs** in Nagrig.

*THANKS, MO!

24

One day, a man called **Reda El-Mallah** came to Nagrig. He was a **football scout** from **Cairo** and he had come to watch a boy called **Sherif.**

Sherif played in a match with **Mo** and all the other boys in Nagrig.

THWACK!

Sherif was good . . . but **Mr El–Mallah** ended up watching Mo, as Mo was the *BEST!*

WHO IS **THAT** KID?

SALAH'S JOURNEY TO **FOOTBALL STARDOM** HAD BEGUN.

First, Mo played for a club in **Tanta,** about **90 minutes'** drive away from Nagrig.

Then, when he was **14,** Mo joined the youth team at **El Mokawloon,** a team in the **Egyptian Premier League.**

To get to his training in **Cairo,** Mo travelled by bus **for more than FOUR HOURS** each way!

The buses were small, hot and crowded. Some of the roads were bumpy and dangerous.

Mo had to **change buses two or three times.**

القاهرة
Cairo
130 km

CRUMP!

31

Mo's typical day:

6:00 am: Breakfast

7:00 am: Start school

9:00 am: Finish school

(He had special permission to finish school early.)

9:30 am: Catch bus

2:00 pm: Arrive in Cairo

Mo's timetable left him tired - **very tired.**
But he was so **determined** to become a
star footballer like his heroes, that all
the travel and hard work was worth it.

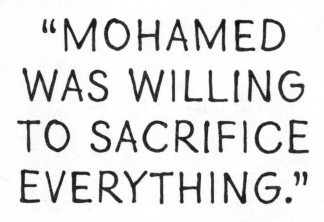

"MOHAMED WAS WILLING TO SACRIFICE EVERYTHING."

Hamdi Nooh, Salah's youth coach

36

CHAPTER 4

CAIRO KID

In the **Egyptian Premier League,** the biggest, most successful clubs are the Cairo teams **Al Ahly** and their fierce rivals **Zamalek.**

But **El Mokawloon** was a great club for young players like Mo to develop.

In the **youth team,** Mo started at **left-back,** but he was not happy.

When the coaches saw how much he wanted to attack, they moved him up to the **right wing.**

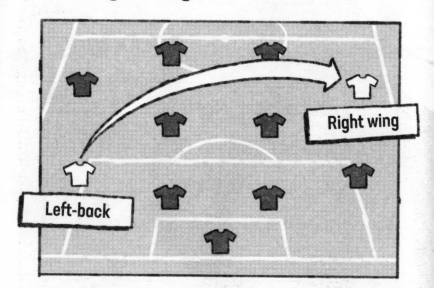

Right wing

Left-back

In his new position, he scored **34 GOALS** in one season. Salah was **smiling again.**

Mo made his **first-team debut** for **El Mokawloon** in **May 2010.** The club had given him a contract - and a **room near the stadium.**

NO MORE *BUS JOURNEYS* FOR *MO!*

El Mokawloon Stadium

The club had signed another Mo, too!
Mohamed Elneny was the same age as
Salah and they became **great friends**.

Mohamed Elneny
(Arsenal midfielder)

FIRST GOAL

25 DECEMBER 2010

EGYPTIAN PREMIER LEAGUE

AL AHLY 1-1 EL MOKAWLOON

El Mokawloon were **away at Cairo giants Al Ahly.** It was a big match!

Early in the second half, **Mohamed Adel** played a long ball down the left and Salah was off!

After a **speedy run,** a brilliant **first touch** and a superb **left-footed shot,** he scored a . . .

Mo kissed the pitch. It was his **first senior goal** - and there were lots more to come!

SALAH'S EL MOKAWLOON RECORD

APPEARANCES	GOALS	ASSISTS
44	12	6

El Mokawloon are also known as **Arab Contractors,** after the company that founded the club.

CHAPTER 5

EGYPTIAN KING

As Mo began to **shine** at his club, he started to play for **Egypt,** too.

In **2011,** he travelled to **Colombia** to play in the **Under-20 World Cup.**

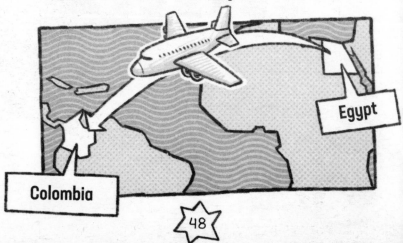

Egypt

Colombia

They were **unbeaten** in a group that included tournament favourites, **Brazil!**

Egypt lost their **knockout game** against **Argentina,** but Mo scored a penalty!

In **2012,** Egypt played at the **London Olympics.** It was an incredible honour - and very exciting for Salah.

They were in a group with *Brazil* again!

50

Mo scored **THREE** goals - one in each of Egypt's group games.

In **October 2011,** Mo scored his **first goal** for the **senior Egypt team** in an **Africa Cup of Nations** qualifier against **Niger.**

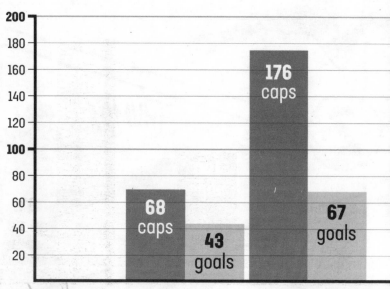

MOHAMED SALAH
2011-

HOSSAM HASSAN
1985-2006

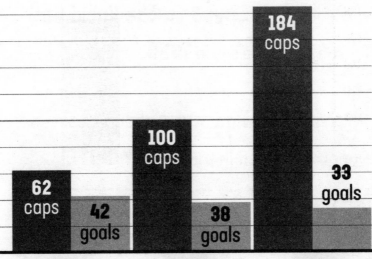

COULD HE BECOME EGYPT'S ALL-TIME *TOP SCORER?*

62 caps · **42** goals

100 caps · **38** goals

184 caps · **33** goals

HASSAN EL SHAZLY
1961-1975

MOHAMED ABOU TRIKA
2001-2013

AHMED HASSAN
1995-2012

8 OCTOBER 2017

WORLD CUP QUALIFIER

EGYPT 2-1 CONGO

This was a crucial **qualifying match** - a win would take **Egypt to the World Cup** for the first time since **1990.**

Salah put **The Pharaohs** ahead, but then Congo equalised in the **87th MINUTE!**

Then - in injury time - Egypt had a penalty.

Mo stepped up to take it . . .

AND SCORED!

The crowd - and the **whole of Egypt** -

went wild.

SALAH WAS A **NATIONAL HERO.**

SALAH! SALAH!

Salah is the **best _Egyptian_ player,** but how does he compare with some other players from the rest of **AFRICA?**

RIYAD MAHREZ

ALGERIA / MANCHESTER CITY

CLUB GOALS **109**

INTERNATIONAL GOALS **16**

SADIO MANÉ

SENEGAL / LIVERPOOL

CLUB GOALS **158**

INTERNATIONAL GOALS **19**

PIERRE-EMERICK AUBAMEYANG

GABON / ARSENAL

CLUB GOALS **270**

INTERNATIONAL GOALS **25**

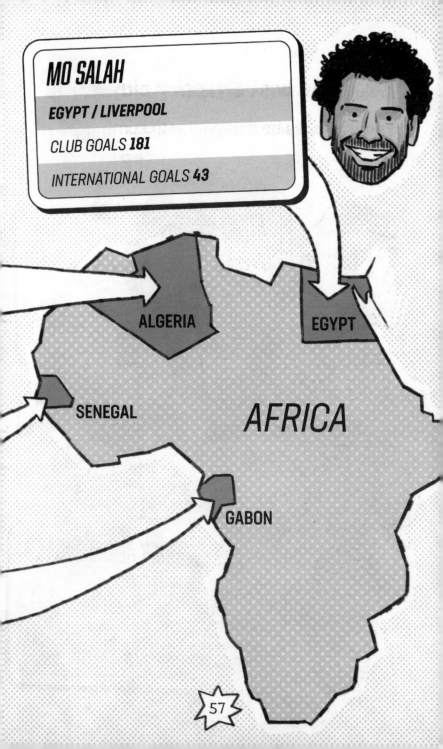

Salah has won the **African Footballer of the Year Award** twice - in **2017** and **2018**.

58

He came **second in 2019,** when his Liverpool **team-mate** Sadio Mané was the winner!

FOOTBALL NEWS

AFRICAN FOOTBALLER OF THE YEAR 2019

SALAH'S EGYPT RECORD

CAPS	GOALS	ASSISTS
68	43	22

Salah was not fully fit at the **2018 World Cup**, but he still scored two goals.

CHAPTER 6

MO ON THE MOVE

61

In **2012**, Mo was the **most exciting** player in **Egypt.** The big clubs, **Zamalek** and **Al Ahly** both wanted to sign him.

But the **El Mokawloon** coaches told Mo that he was **way too good** to play in the **Egyptian league**.

YOU SHOULD PLAY IN EUROPE.

YOU COULD BE A REAL **STAR.**

Problems in Egypt meant that the **2011–12 season** ended early, so it was a good time to move on.

Over 4,000 kilometres away, in **Switzerland**, a club called **Basel** had seen Mo play. They invited the **Egypt under-23 side** to play a friendly in March 2012.

Salah's **speedy runs, swerving dribbles** and **TWO GOALS** wowed the Basel bosses.

In **June 2012**, Basel **signed** Mo for

£2.25 MILLION!

Bargain!

Switzerland is **very different** from Egypt. Mo had to learn a new language and make new friends.

But it was easier for Salah when his friend **Mohamed Elneny** signed for Basel in January 2013!

As one of the **best Swiss clubs,** Basel regularly qualified for the **Champions League** or **Europa League.** Mo would play against some of the **top teams in Europe!**

11 APRIL 2013

EUROPA LEAGUE QUARTER-FINAL 2ND LEG

BASEL 4-4 TOTTENHAM (4-1 ON PENALTIES)

Salah scored his **first Europa League goal** as Basel beat Spurs and set up a semi-final against **Chelsea**.

Salah **scored against Chelsea** in the second leg of the semi-final.

But Basel lost.

In the **2013–14 season,** Basel qualified for the **Champions League.** They were drawn in the same group as . . . **Chelsea!**

18 SEPTEMBER 2013

CHAMPIONS LEAGUE GROUP STAGE

CHELSEA 1-2 BASEL

*Basel were trailing until **Salah scored.** And then they scored again and **won!***

26 NOVEMBER 2013

CHAMPIONS LEAGUE GROUP STAGE

BASEL 1-0 CHELSEA

Salah was on fire and scored the winning goal in the 87th minute.

BOOM!

THIS SALAH GUY KEEPS SCORING AGAINST US. **LET'S SIGN HIM!**

José Mourinho,
Chelsea manager
(2004-07 and 2013-15)

Liverpool wanted to sign him, too.

So, after **two seasons** with Basel, Salah **signed for Chelsea** for an estimated

£11 MILLION!

Salah scored his first Chelsea goal in a **6-0 demolition of Arsenal,** but then . . .

. . . at the start of the **2014–15 season** he lost his confidence and stopped scoring goals.

Mourinho picked other players before Salah.

SORRY, MO.

LAH

It didn't really work out for Mo at Chelsea.

But Salah didn't want to sit on the **substitute bench.**

HE NEEDED TO PLAY **FOOTBALL!**

SALAH'S BASEL RECORD

APPEARANCES	GOALS	ASSISTS
79	20	17

Salah won two **Swiss League** titles with **Basel**.

SALAH'S CHELSEA RECORD

APPEARANCES	GOALS	ASSISTS
19	2	4

In **February 2015,** Salah was on the move again. **Chelsea** sent him **on loan** to **Fiorentina**, based in the beautiful city of **Florence, Italy.**

Florence was home to genius artists, such as Michelangelo and Leonardo da Vinci!

DAVID
MICHELANGELO

Mo scored against **Tottenham** in the **Europa League** and **Inter Milan** in **Serie A**. He also netted **TWO brilliant goals** against **Juventus** in the **Coppa Italia**.

CRACK!

SALAH WAS BACK ON FORM!

Chelsea didn't need Mo back at the end of the season, so he **moved on loan** to another Italian club - **AS Roma.**

AS Roma's home is in the Italian city of *Rome.*

BEEP! BEEP!

The Colosseum, famous Rome landmark

Mo would play alongside striker **Edin Džeko,** who was on loan from **Manchester City.**

Plus, **Roma legend** and Mo's **all-time hero, Francesco Totti** was still at the club.

IT WAS A DREAM MOVE!

After a successful season on loan, in 2016 Salah signed for Roma for **£13.5 MILLION.**

ROMA HIGHLIGHTS

SOME OF THE BIGGEST GAMES
FROM SALAH'S TIME IN ROME.

25 OCTOBER 2015

SERIE A

FIORENTINA 1-2 ROMA

Salah scored his **FIFTH goal** in **SIX Serie A**
games on this visit to his former club.
But . . . he was then **sent off** for the first
(and so far, only) time in his career.

4 NOVEMBER 2015

CHAMPIONS LEAGUE GROUP STAGE

ROMA 3-2 BAYER LEVERKUSEN

Mo **scored one goal** and **assisted another** as the German side were beaten in the Champions League.

Salah was **Roma's top scorer** in his first season, with **15 goals**.

He was also voted *Player of the Season.*

6 NOVEMBER 2016

SERIE A

ROMA 3-0 BOLOGNA

Salah **scored all three goals** in this win - his first ever career **hat-trick** at club level.

SALAH'S RECORD IN ITALY

FIORENTINA

APPEARANCES	GOALS	ASSISTS
26	9	4

ROMA

APPEARANCES	GOALS	ASSISTS
83	34	22

CHAPTER 8

WELCOME TO LIVERPOOL

In the **summer of 2017,** Salah signed for one of the **biggest and most famous clubs** in the world:

Mo made his Liverpool debut at Watford on the opening day of the **2017–18 Premier League season.**

Sadio Mané scored a goal . . .

POW!

Roberto Firmino scored a penalty . . .

BOFF!

And then - **_BOOM_** - Salah scored one for himself!

That was it - Mo had **started scoring**, and **NOTHING** was going to stop him.

GAMES AND GOALS
2017-18

HIGHLIGHTS FROM AN **INCREDIBLE** DEBUT SEASON.

10 DECEMBER 2017

PREMIER LEAGUE

LIVERPOOL 1-1 EVERTON

A superb **solo goal** in his debut **Merseyside Derby. Perfect!**

This goal won the **Puskas Award** for **best goal** of the season

17 MARCH 2018

PREMIER LEAGUE

LIVERPOOL 5-0 WATFORD

Salah scored **FOUR goals** in this thrashing of Watford. **Awesome!**

4 APRIL 2018

CHAMPIONS LEAGUE QUARTER-FINAL 1ST LEG

LIVERPOOL 3-0 MAN CITY

A brilliant **goal** and an **assist** from Salah.
Mo **scored again** in the **second leg.**

24 APRIL 2018

CHAMPIONS LEAGUE SEMI-FINAL 1ST LEG

LIVERPOOL 5-2 ROMA

Salah's **TWO goals** and **TWO assists** helped
send Liverpool to the Champions League Final.

87

26 MAY 2018

CHAMPIONS LEAGUE FINAL

OLYMPIC STADIUM, KIEV

REAL MADRID 3-1 LIVERPOOL

At the end of an **amazing first season,** Liverpool faced **Real Madrid** in the **Champions League Final.**

A HUGE GAME!

Virgil van Dijk

88

But in the 30th minute, Mo **injured his shoulder** in a **battle for the ball** with Madrid defender **Sergio Ramos.**

Salah couldn't play on and **left the pitch in tears.** Liverpool lost 3-1. It was a **disaster.**

But Salah and his **team-mates** promised themselves they would come back **stronger.**

PREMIER LEAGUE RECORD BREAKER

SALAH'S TOP-FLIGHT RECORDS IN 2017-18

32 GOALS – the most **ever** **scored** in a **38-game** season.

First player to win the

PLAYER OF THE MONTH AWARD

three times in season.

First **African player** to score **30 GOALS** in a **Premier League** season.

First player to score in
24 separate **Premier League** games.

Winning the
GOLDEN BOOT
in his first season.

Awesome!

THE PREMIER LEAGUE STATS

APPEARANCES	GOALS	ASSISTS
36	32	11

LIVERPOOL HIGH SCORERS

Salah's **44 GOALS in all competitions** is a **Liverpool record** for a **debut season**. How does he compare to record seasons for other **Liverpool legends?**

IAN RUSH
1983-84
47 GOALS

ALL-TIME RECORD

THE MAN

MO SALAH
2017-18
44 GOALS

FERNANDO TORRES
2007-08
33 GOALS

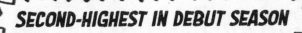

SECOND-HIGHEST IN DEBUT SEASON

ALL COMPETITION STATS

APPEARANCES	GOALS	ASSISTS
52	44	16

SALAH WAS VOTED:

Premier League Player of the Year

Players' Player of the Year

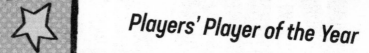

Football Writers' Association
Player of the Year

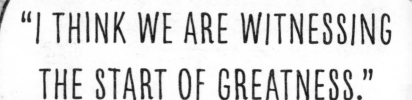

"I THINK WE ARE WITNESSING THE START OF GREATNESS."

Liverpool legend, Steven Gerrard

94

CHAPTER 9

KING OF EUROPE

2018-19 HIGHLIGHTS

> ## HOW WOULD MO TOP HIS SPECTACULAR FIRST SEASON?

24 OCTOBER 2018

CHAMPIONS LEAGUE GROUP STAGE

LIVERPOOL 4-0 RED STAR BELGRADE

*The second of Salah's **TWO GOALS** was his **50th for Liverpool** as the Reds cruised past the Serbian side.*

8 DECEMBER 2018

PREMIER LEAGUE

BOURNEMOUTH 0-4 LIVERPOOL

In a **pre-Christmas trip** to the **south coast,** Salah gifted the Liverpool fans with his **second hat-trick** for the club.

26 APRIL 2019

PREMIER LEAGUE

LIVERPOOL 5-0 HUDDERSFIELD TOWN

Salah marked his **100TH APPEARANCE** for Liverpool with **TWO GOALS. Fantastic!**

97

TIGHT TITLE RACE!

Liverpool, and their rivals, **Manchester City,** had been fighting for the title all season.

In the end, City won it on the final day - by **just one point!**

POSITION	TEAM	POINTS
1	MANCHESTER CITY	98
2	LIVERPOOL	97
3	CHELSEA	72
4	TOTTENHAM HOTSPUR	71
5	ARSENAL	70
6	MANCHESTER UNITED	66

IT WAS SO CLOSE!

Salah didn't win the title, but he did score **22 PREMIER LEAGUE** goals!

He was the league's joint top-scorer and shared the **GOLDEN BOOT** with team-mate **Sadio Mané** and **Arsenal** striker **Pierre-Emerick Aubameyang.**

EUROPEAN DREAMS

1 JUNE 2019

CHAMPIONS LEAGUE FINAL

WANDA METROPOLITANO, MADRID

LIVERPOOL 2-0 TOTTENHAM HOTSPUR

Liverpool had made it to the **Champions League final** – this time against **Tottenham Hotspur.**

Liverpool were awarded a **penalty** in the **FIRST MINUTE** of the game. Mo stepped up to take it and ... *BOOM* – the ball was in the back of the net!

100

After **Divock Origi** added a second goal late on, Liverpool were the

CHAMPIONS OF EUROPE.

Mo had **forgotten the disappointment against Madrid** and his **bus journeys to Cairo** seemed like a different world.

SALAH'S 2018-19 RECORD

APPEARANCES	GOALS	ASSISTS
52	27	12

Salah is the **fastest Liverpool** player to reach **50 Premier League goals.**

And he has scored the **most goals (69)** after **100 Liverpool appearances.**

CHAPTER 10

LEAGUE CHAMPIONS!

2019-20 HIGHLIGHTS

SALAH'S BEST BITS OF A VERY UNUSUAL SEASON.

9 AUGUST 2019

PREMIER LEAGUE

LIVERPOOL 4-1 NORWICH CITY

Salah and Liverpool started the **new season with a bang.** Mo scored one goal and assisted another as **Norwich were thrashed.**

21 DECEMBER 2019

CLUB WORLD CUP FINAL

LIVERPOOL 1-0 FLAMENGO

Liverpool won the **Club World Cup** for the first time in their history – they were the best club in the world! Salah was voted **Best Player of the Tournament.**

19 JANUARY 2020

PREMIER LEAGUE

LIVERPOOL 2-0 MANCHESTER UTD

Salah picked up a long clearance from keeper **Alisson** to score a brilliant goal against their old rivals.

In **March 2020,** Liverpool were **25 POINTS** clear at the top of the league. But then, the unthinkable happened - all football stopped because of the **Coronavirus lockdown.**

BREAKING NEWS

FOOTBALL SUPERSTARS NEWS

FOOTBALL CANCELLED

FOOTBALL is taking a break. Stay safe everybody!

The fans anxiously waited and hoped. Would the league start again?

In June, football came back - but the fans had to stay at home.

WOMP!

COOO! GREAT GOAL MO!

Pigeon fans were still allowed!

On **25 June 2020**, **Chelsea** beat **Manchester City.** It meant that nobody could catch **Liverpool** - they had won the **Premier League** with a record-breaking **SEVEN games** to go!

IT WAS LIVERPOOL'S FIRST LEAGUE TITLE FOR 30 YEARS.

Salah had won the **Champions League** last season and now he was a **Premier League winner.**

INCREDIBLE!

Salah, along with **Sadio Mané** and **Roberto Firmino** are one of the world's most **lethal attacking trios.**

Sadio Mané

Roberto Firmino

In **July 2020,** when Mo scored two goals against Brighton, it meant that between them, **Salah,** Mané and Firmino had scored **250 GOALS** while **Jürgen Klopp** was in charge.

GREAT WORK, GUYS

SALAH'S 2019-20 RECORD

APPEARANCES	GOALS	ASSISTS
48	23	13

Salah was Liverpool's **top scorer** in 2019-20.

Mohamed Salah **23 GOALS**

Sadio Mané **22 GOALS**

Roberto Firmino **12 GOALS**

Great goals like the ones Salah scores need **great celebrations.** Mo has a few:

THE YOGA MAN

THE EGYPTIAN KING

THE PRAYER

In his spare time, Mo likes to relax by

. . . doing some **yoga.**

. . . playing **video games.**

And he loves beating **team-mate Dejan Lovren** at **table tennis!**

Mo Salah is now **one of the most famous people on the planet.**

In 2019, **TIME magazine** named Salah as one of the **World's 100 most influential people.**

There is even a mural of him in **Times Square** in **New York City.**

He's been called *"The Egyptian Messi".*

Salah has never forgotten where he came from. The young boy who fed stray dogs in **Nagrig** has gone on to donate **MILLIONS to charities in Egypt** and around the world.

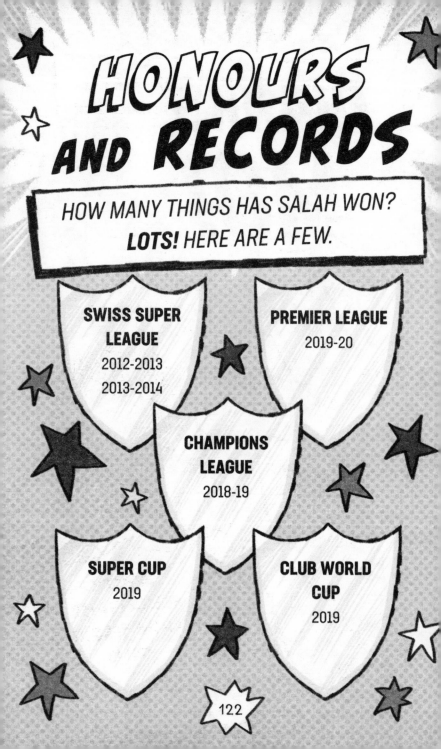

QUIZ TIME!

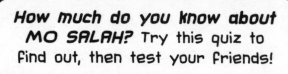

How much do you know about **MO SALAH?** Try this quiz to find out, then test your friends!

1. What was Salah's first professional club?

----

2. Which Italian forward was one of Salah's heroes when he was a boy?

----

3. How long did it take Mo to get to training in Cairo by bus?

----

4. Mo scored the penalty that sent Egypt to the 2018 World Cup. Which country was it against?

----

5. Which Swiss team did Salah sign for in 2012?

---

6. Which team signed Mo after he scored against them in three games?

---

7. How much did Roma sign Salah for in 2016?

---

8. How many goals did Mo score for Liverpool in his debut season?

---

9. Which team did Liverpool beat in the 2019 Champions League final?

---

10. How many times has Salah won the Premier League Golden Boot?

The answers are on the next page *but no peeking!*

ANSWERS

1. El Mokawloon
2. Francesco Totti
3. Four hours
4. Congo
5. Basel
6. Chelsea
7. £13.5 million
8. 44
9. Tottenham Hotspur
10. Two

MO SALAH:
WORDS YOU NEED TO KNOW

Premier League
The top football league in England.

Africa Cup of Nations
The main international football competition in Africa.

PFA
Professional Footballers' Association

FWA
Football Writers' Association

Serie A
The top football league in the Netherlands.

Champions League
European club competition held every year. The winner is the best team in Europe.

Europa League
The second-tier European club competition.

ABOUT THE AUTHORS

Simon's first job was at the Science Museum, making paper aeroplanes and blowing bubbles big enough for your dad to stand in. Since then he's written all sorts of books about the stuff he likes, from dinosaurs and rockets, to llamas, loud music and of course, football. Simon has supported Ipswich Town since they won the FA Cup in 1978 (it's true - look it up) and once sat next to Rio Ferdinand on a train. He lives in Kent with his wife and daughter, two tortoises and a cat.

Dan has drawn silly pictures since he could hold a crayon. Then he grew up and started making books about stuff like trucks, space, people's jobs, *Doctor Who* and *Star Wars*. Dan remembers Ipswich Town winning the FA Cup but he didn't watch it because he was too busy making a Viking ship out of brown paper. As a result, he knows more about Vikings than football. Dan lives in Suffolk with his wife, son, daughter and a dog that takes him for very long walks.